MW01485298

Contents

All About Me

Year	Age

I'm really good at . . .

Style	Move
Jump	Leap
Turn	

This years favorites!

Costume	Hair Do / Wig
Music	Choreography
Style	Move
Teacher	Class

If I could change something this year, I would change . . .

This year I want to learn how to . . . .

This year we learned . . .

All About My Team

Funniest Teammate	Most Talkative
Most Supportive	Hardest Worker
Best at Leaps	Best at Turns

My Best Dance Friends

What I love about my team

Together we love to . . .

Dance Team / Style	Song	Teacher

Costumes!

Year

photo

Team	
Style	
Song	

Team	
Style	
Song	

photo

photo

Team	
Style	
Song	

Costumes!

Year

photo

Song | Style | Team

photo

Team

Style

Song

photo

Team	
Style	
Song	

Costumes!

Year

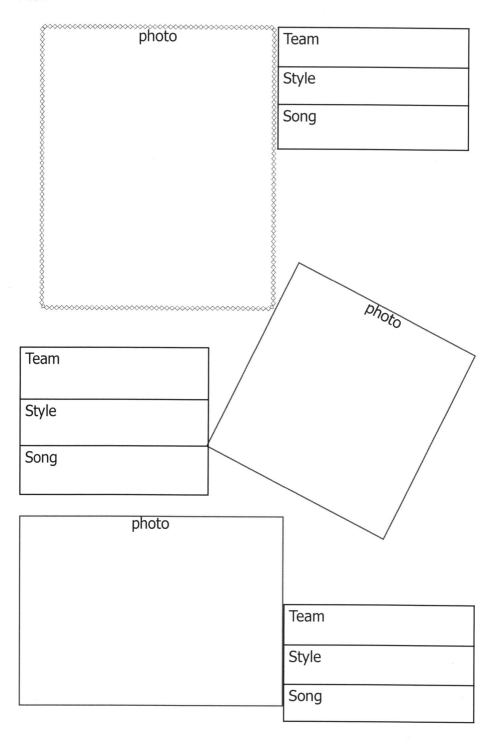

photo

Team	
Style	
Song	

Team

Style

Song

photo

Team

Style

Song

photo

Team	
Style	
Song	

Costumes!

Year

photo

Song	Style	Team

photo

Team	
Style	
Song	

photo

Team	
Style	
Song	

All About Me

Year	Age

I'm really good at . . .

Style	Move
Jump	Leap
Turn	

This years favorites!

Costume	Hair Do / Wig
Music	Choreography
Style	Move
Teacher	Class

If I could change something this year, I would change . . .

This year I want to learn how to . . . .

This year we learned . . .

All About My Team

Funniest Teammate	Most Talkative
Most Supportive	Hardest Worker
Best at Leaps	Best at Turns

My Best Dance Friends

What I love about my team

Together we love to . . .

Dance Team / Style	Song	Teacher

Costumes!

Year

photo

Team	
Style	
Song	

photo

Team	
Style	
Song	

photo

Team	
Style	
Song	

Costumes!

Year

photo

Team	Style	Song

photo

Team	Style	Song

photo

Team
Style
Song

Costumes!

Year

photo

Team
Style
Song

Team
Style
Song

photo

photo

Team
Style
Song

Costumes!

Year

photo

Song	Style	Team

photo

Team	
Style	
Song	

photo

Team	
Style	
Song	

All About Me

Year	Age

I'm really good at . . .

Style	Move
Jump	Leap
Turn	

This years favorites!

Costume	Hair Do / Wig
Music	Choreography
Style	Move
Teacher	Class

If I could change something this year, I would change . . .

This year I want to learn how to . . . .

This year we learned . . .

All About My Team

Funniest Teammate	Most Talkative
Most Supportive	Hardest Worker
Best at Leaps	Best at Turns

My Best Dance Friends

What I love about my team

Together we love to . . .

Dance Team / Style	Song	Teacher

Costumes!

Year

photo

Team
Style
Song

photo

Team
Style
Song

photo

Team
Style
Song

Costumes!

Year

photo

Song	Style	Team

photo

Team	
Style	
Song	

photo

Team	
Style	
Song	

Costumes!

Year

photo

Team	
Style	
Song	

Team	
Style	
Song	

photo

photo

Team	
Style	
Song	

Costumes!

Year

photo

Song	Style	Team

photo

Team
Style
Song

photo

Team
Style
Song

Competition						Date	
Location							

Dance	Division	Results

I Feel like I did . . .	I Smiled	Pointed Toes	Straight Legs	In step	With the music
THE BEST EVER!					
Better than last time					
OK, The same					
ugh, I'll do better next time					

What I THINK the judges will say . . .	What the judges DID say . . .

We did GREAT!   Especially . . . .

Next time we need to . . .

I couldn't have done it with out the help of . . .

Competition			Date
Location			

Dance	Division	Results

I Feel like I did . . .	I Smiled	Pointed Toes	Straight Legs	In step	With the music
THE BEST EVER!					
Better than last time					
OK, The same					
ugh, I'll do better next time					

What I THINK
the judges will say . . .

What the judges
DID say . . .

We did GREAT!   Especially . . . .

Next time we need to . . .

I couldn't have done it with out the help of . . .

Competition					Date	
Location						
Dance	Division		Results			

I Feel like I did . . .	I Smiled	Pointed Toes	Straight Legs	In step	With the music
THE BEST EVER!					
Better than last time					
OK, The same					
ugh, I'll do better next time					

What I THINK
the judges will say . . .

What the judges
DID say . . .

We did GREAT!   Especially . . . .

Next time we need to . . .

I couldn't have done it with out the help of . . .

Competition		Date
Location		

Dance	Division	Results

I Feel like I did . . .	I Smiled	Pointed Toes	Straight Legs	In step	With the music
THE BEST EVER!					
Better than last time					
OK, The same					
ugh, I'll do better next time					

What I THINK the judges will say . . .	What the judges DID say . . .

We did GREAT!   Especially . . . .

Next time we need to . . .

I couldn't have done it with out the help of . . .

Competition		Date
Location		

Dance	Division	Results

I Feel like I did . . .	I Smiled	Pointed Toes	Straight Legs	In step	With the music
THE BEST EVER!					
Better than last time					
OK, The same					
ugh, I'll do better next time					

What I THINK the judges will say . . .	What the judges DID say . . .

We did GREAT! Especially . . . .

Next time we need to . . .

I couldn't have done it with out the help of . . .

Competition						Date	
Location							

Dance	Division	Results					

I Feel like I did . . .	I Smiled	Pointed Toes	Straight Legs	In step	With the music
THE BEST EVER!					
Better than last time					
OK, The same					
ugh, I'll do better next time					

What I THINK the judges will say . . .	What the judges DID say . . .

We did GREAT!   Especially . . . .

Next time we need to . . .

I couldn't have done it with out the help of . . .

Competition							Date	
Location								
Dance	Division			Results				

I Feel like I did . . .	I Smiled	Pointed Toes	Straight Legs	In step	With the music
THE BEST EVER!					
Better than last time					
OK, The same					
ugh, I'll do better next time					

What I THINK
the judges will say . . .

What the judges
DID say . . .

We did GREAT!   Especially . . . .

Next time we need to . . .

I couldn't have done it with out the help of . . .

Competition			Date		
Location					

Dance	Division	Results			

I Feel like I did . . .	I Smiled	Pointed Toes	Straight Legs	In step	With the music
THE BEST EVER!					
Better than last time					
OK, The same					
ugh, I'll do better next time					

What I THINK the judges will say . . .	What the judges DID say . . .

We did GREAT! Especially . . . .

Next time we need to . . .

I couldn't have done it with out the help of . . .

Competition		Date
Location		

Dance	Division	Results

I Feel like I did . . .	I Smiled	Pointed Toes	Straight Legs	In step	With the music
THE BEST EVER!					
Better than last time					
OK, The same					
ugh, I'll do better next time					

What I THINK
the judges will say . . .

What the judges
DID say . . .

We did GREAT!   Especially . . . .

Next time we need to . . .

I couldn't have done it with out the help of . . .

Competition		Date	
Location			

Dance	Division	Results

I Feel like I did . . .	I Smiled	Pointed Toes	Straight Legs	In step	With the music
THE BEST EVER!					
Better than last time					
OK, The same					
ugh, I'll do better next time					

What I THINK the judges will say . . .	What the judges DID say . . .

We did GREAT!   Especially . . . .

Next time we need to . . .

I couldn't have done it with out the help of . . .

Competition		Date
Location		

Dance	Division	Results

I Feel like I did . . .	I Smiled	Pointed Toes	Straight Legs	In step	With the music
THE BEST EVER!					
Better than last time					
OK, The same					
ugh, I'll do better next time					

What I THINK
the judges will say . . .

What the judges
DID say . . .

We did GREAT!   Especially . . . .

Next time we need to . . .

I couldn't have done it with out the help of . . .

Competition		Date
Location		

Dance	Division	Results

I Feel like I did . . .	I Smiled	Pointed Toes	Straight Legs	In step	With the music
THE BEST EVER!					
Better than last time					
OK, The same					
ugh, I'll do better next time					

What I THINK the judges will say . . .	What the judges DID say . . .

We did GREAT!   Especially . . . .

Next time we need to . . .

I couldn't have done it with out the help of . . .

Competition		Date
Location		

Dance	Division	Results

I Feel like I did . . .	I Smiled	Pointed Toes	Straight Legs	In step	With the music
THE BEST EVER!					
Better than last time					
OK, The same					
ugh, I'll do better next time					

What I THINK
the judges will say . . .

What the judges
DID say . . .

We did GREAT!   Especially . . . .

Next time we need to . . .

I couldn't have done it with out the help of . . .

Competition		Date	
Location			
Dance	Division	Results	

I Feel like I did . . .	I Smiled	Pointed Toes	Straight Legs	In step	With the music
THE BEST EVER!					
Better than last time					
OK, The same					
ugh, I'll do better next time					

What I THINK the judges will say . . .	What the judges DID say . . .

We did GREAT!   Especially . . . .

Next time we need to . . .

I couldn't have done it with out the help of . . .

Competition		Date
Location		

Dance	Division	Results

I Feel like I did . . .	I Smiled	Pointed Toes	Straight Legs	In step	With the music
THE BEST EVER!					
Better than last time					
OK, The same					
ugh, I'll do better next time					

What I THINK the judges will say . . .	What the judges DID say . . .

We did GREAT!   Especially . . . .

Next time we need to . . .

I couldn't have done it with out the help of . . .

Competition		Date
Location		

Dance	Division	Results

I Feel like I did . . .	I Smiled	Pointed Toes	Straight Legs	In step	With the music
THE BEST EVER!					
Better than last time					
OK, The same					
ugh, I'll do better next time					

What I THINK the judges will say . . .	What the judges DID say . . .

We did GREAT!   Especially . . . .

Next time we need to . . .

I couldn't have done it with out the help of . . .

Competition		Date
Location		

Dance	Division	Results

I Feel like I did . . .	I Smiled	Pointed Toes	Straight Legs	In step	With the music
THE BEST EVER!					
Better than last time					
OK, The same					
ugh, I'll do better next time					

What I THINK
the judges will say . . .

What the judges
DID say . . .

We did GREAT!   Especially . . . .

Next time we need to . . .

I couldn't have done it with out the help of . . .

Competition		Date
Location		

Dance	Division	Results

I Feel like I did . . .	I Smiled	Pointed Toes	Straight Legs	In step	With the music
THE BEST EVER!					
Better than last time					
OK, The same					
ugh, I'll do better next time					

What I THINK the judges will say . . .	What the judges DID say . . .

We did GREAT!   Especially . . . .

Next time we need to . . .

I couldn't have done it with out the help of . . .

Competition		Date
Location		

Dance	Division	Results

I Feel like I did . . .	I Smiled	Pointed Toes	Straight Legs	In step	With the music
THE BEST EVER!					
Better than last time					
OK, The same					
ugh, I'll do better next time					

What I THINK the judges will say . . .	What the judges DID say . . .

We did GREAT!   Especially . . . .

Next time we need to . . .

I couldn't have done it with out the help of . . .

Competition		Date
Location		

Dance	Division	Results

I Feel like I did . . .	I Smiled	Pointed Toes	Straight Legs	In step	With the music
THE BEST EVER!					
Better than last time					
OK, The same					
ugh, I'll do better next time					

What I THINK
the judges will say . . .

What the judges
DID say . . .

We did GREAT!   Especially . . . .

Next time we need to . . .

I couldn't have done it with out the help of . . .

Competition		Date
Location		

Dance	Division	Results

I Feel like I did . . .	I Smiled	Pointed Toes	Straight Legs	In step	With the music
THE BEST EVER!					
Better than last time					
OK, The same					
ugh, I'll do better next time					

What I THINK the judges will say . . .	What the judges DID say . . .

We did GREAT! Especially . . . .

Next time we need to . . .

I couldn't have done it with out the help of . . .

Competition		Date
Location		

Dance	Division	Results

I Feel like I did . . .	I Smiled	Pointed Toes	Straight Legs	In step	With the music
THE BEST EVER!					
Better than last time					
OK, The same					
ugh, I'll do better next time					

What I THINK
the judges will say . . .

What the judges
DID say . . .

We did GREAT!   Especially . . . .

Next time we need to . . .

I couldn't have done it with out the help of . . .

Competition		Date	
Location			

Dance	Division	Results

I Feel like I did . . .	I Smiled	Pointed Toes	Straight Legs	In step	With the music
THE BEST EVER!					
Better than last time					
OK, The same					
ugh, I'll do better next time					

What I THINK
the judges will say . . .

What the judges
DID say . . .

We did GREAT!   Especially . . . .

Next time we need to . . .

I couldn't have done it with out the help of . . .

Competition				Date	
Location					

Dance	Division	Results			

I Feel like I did . . .	I Smiled	Pointed Toes	Straight Legs	In step	With the music
THE BEST EVER!					
Better than last time					
OK, The same					
ugh, I'll do better next time					

What I THINK the judges will say . . .	What the judges DID say . . .

We did GREAT!   Especially . . . .

Next time we need to . . .

I couldn't have done it with out the help of . . .

Competition		Date
Location		

Dance	Division	Results

I Feel like I did . . .	I Smiled	Pointed Toes	Straight Legs	In step	With the music
THE BEST EVER!					
Better than last time					
OK, The same					
ugh, I'll do better next time					

What I THINK the judges will say . . .	What the judges DID say . . .

We did GREAT!   Especially . . . .

Next time we need to . . .

I couldn't have done it with out the help of . . .

Competition		Date
Location		

Dance	Division	Results

I Feel like I did . . .	I Smiled	Pointed Toes	Straight Legs	In step	With the music
THE BEST EVER!					
Better than last time					
OK, The same					
ugh, I'll do better next time					

What I THINK the judges will say . . .	What the judges DID say . . .

We did GREAT!   Especially . . . .

Next time we need to . . .

I couldn't have done it with out the help of . . .

Competition		Date
Location		

Dance	Division	Results

I Feel like I did . . .	I Smiled	Pointed Toes	Straight Legs	In step	With the music
THE BEST EVER!					
Better than last time					
OK, The same					
ugh, I'll do better next time					

What I THINK the judges will say . . .	What the judges DID say . . .

We did GREAT!   Especially . . . .

Next time we need to . . .

I couldn't have done it with out the help of . . .

Competition		Date
Location		

Dance	Division	Results

I Feel like I did . . .	I Smiled	Pointed Toes	Straight Legs	In step	With the music
THE BEST EVER!					
Better than last time					
OK, The same					
ugh, I'll do better next time					

What I THINK
the judges will say . . .

What the judges
DID say . . .

We did GREAT!   Especially . . . .

Next time we need to . . .

I couldn't have done it with out the help of . . .

Competition		Date
Location		

Dance	Division	Results

I Feel like I did . . .	I Smiled	Pointed Toes	Straight Legs	In step	With the music
THE BEST EVER!					
Better than last time					
OK, The same					
ugh, I'll do better next time					

What I THINK
the judges will say . . .

What the judges
DID say . . .

We did GREAT!   Especially . . . .

Next time we need to . . .

I couldn't have done it with out the help of . . .

Competition		Date
Location		

Dance	Division	Results

I Feel like I did . . .	I Smiled	Pointed Toes	Straight Legs	In step	With the music
THE BEST EVER!					
Better than last time					
OK, The same					
ugh, I'll do better next time					

What I THINK
the judges will say . . .

What the judges
DID say . . .

We did GREAT!   Especially . . . .

Next time we need to . . .

I couldn't have done it with out the help of . . .

CONTACTS

Name	Phone	Email	Parents Name

CONTACTS

Name	Phone	Email	Parents Name

MY DANCE STUDIO

ADDRESS

PHONE NUMBER

FAX

EMAIL

WEB ADDRESS

What I love about my Dance Studio . . .
What I love about Dancing . . .
What I love about Competing

ALSO FROM DEBORAH SEVILLA & DREAM BELIEVE ACHIEVE ATHLETICS

ACROBATIC GYMNASTICS

ATHLETE JOURNAL

BASEBALL SCOREBOOK & JOURNAL

COACH EDITIONS WOMEN'S & MEN'S ARTISTIC GYMNASTICS

COMPETITIVE DANCE JOURNAL

GYMNASTICS WORKBOOK

MARTIAL ART BELT BOOK & JOURNAL

MARTIAL ARTS COMPETITIVE JOURNAL

MEN'S ARTISTIC GYMNASTICS SCOREBOOKS & JOURNALS

PARENT'S GUIDE COMPETITIVE GYMNASTICS

RHYTHMIC GYMNASTICS

SOFTBALL SCOREBOOK & JOUNAL

WOMEN'S ARTISTIC GYMNASTICS SCOREBOOKS, JOURNALS

COMING SOON

COLLEGE WORKBOOK

PRINCESS BALLET WORKBOOK

AVAILABLE ON AMAZON.COM

WWW.DBAATHLETICS.COM

IMAGE ON THE COVER OF THIS COMPETITION DANCE JOURNAL IS DESIGNED IN PART BY FREEPIK

COLLEGE WORKBOOK

DEBORAH SEVILLA

Martial Arts
Belt Journal

Deborah Sevilla

DREAM
BELIEVE
ACHIEVE
ATHLETICS

WWW.DBAATHLETICS.COM

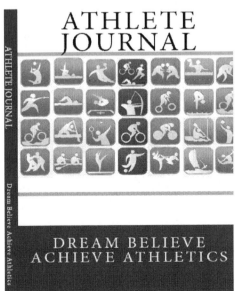

ATHLETE
JOURNAL

ATHLETE JOURNAL

Dream Believe Achieve Athletics

DREAM BELIEVE
ACHIEVE ATHLETICS

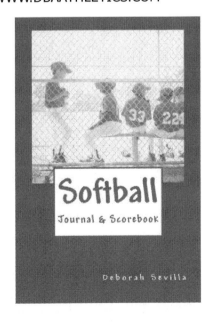

Softball
Journal & Scorebook

Deborah Sevilla

Made in the USA
Columbia, SC
14 May 2022

60424389R00048